KU-466-966

This Hole, That Hole

Written by Seon-hye Jang
Illustrated by Yeong-soon Kim
Edited by Joy Cowley

There is a hole in the tree.
What made the hole?

C00 774 840X

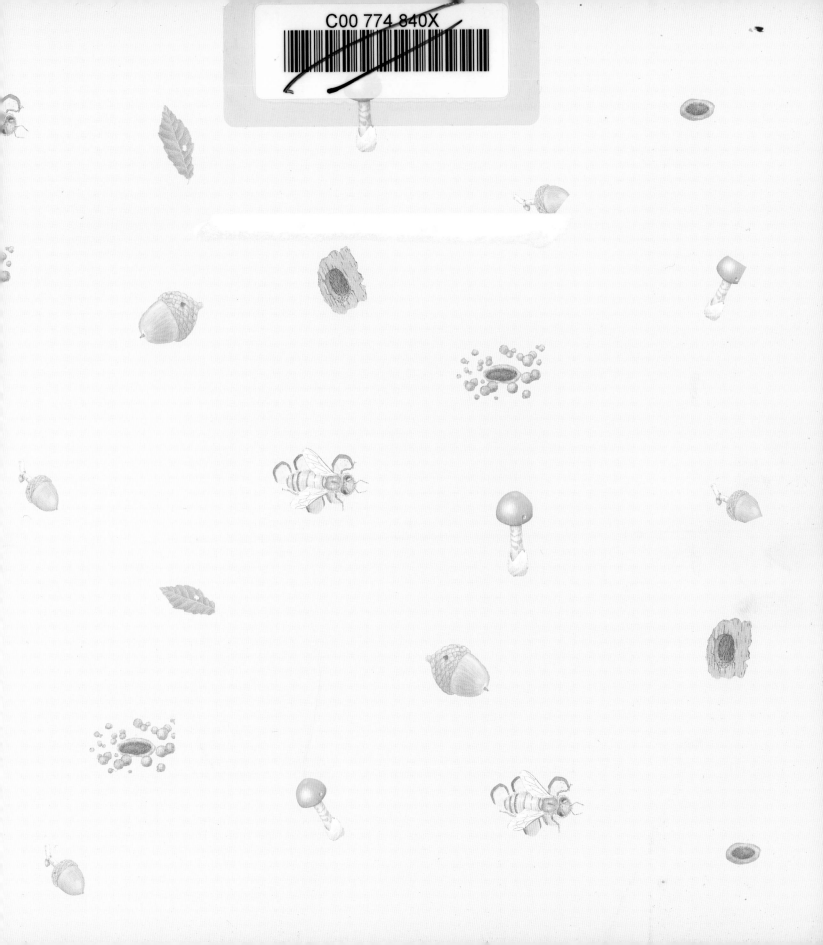

LEISURE AND CULTURE DUNDEE	
C00774840X	
Bertrams	15/11/2016
	£6.99
CC	

big & SMALL

Original Korean text by Seon-hye Jang
Illustrations by Yeong-soon Kim
Korean edition © Aram Publishing

This English edition published by big & SMALL in 2016
by arrangement with Aram Publishing
English text edited by Joy Cowley
English edition © big & SMALL 2016

All rights reserved
ISBN: 978-1-925234-54-1
Printed in Korea

A woodpecker made the hole
to get the grub inside.

6

A hole made by a woodpecker's beak.

7

This hole, that hole!
What made these holes?

These holes were made
by the mouths of insects.
Nibble, nibble.

A hole made by a sow bug

A hole made by a leaf-rolling weevil

A hole is in the bark.
A hole is in the acorn.
Why are these holes here?

These holes were made
for laying eggs.
The eggs will hatch
and grow in the holes.

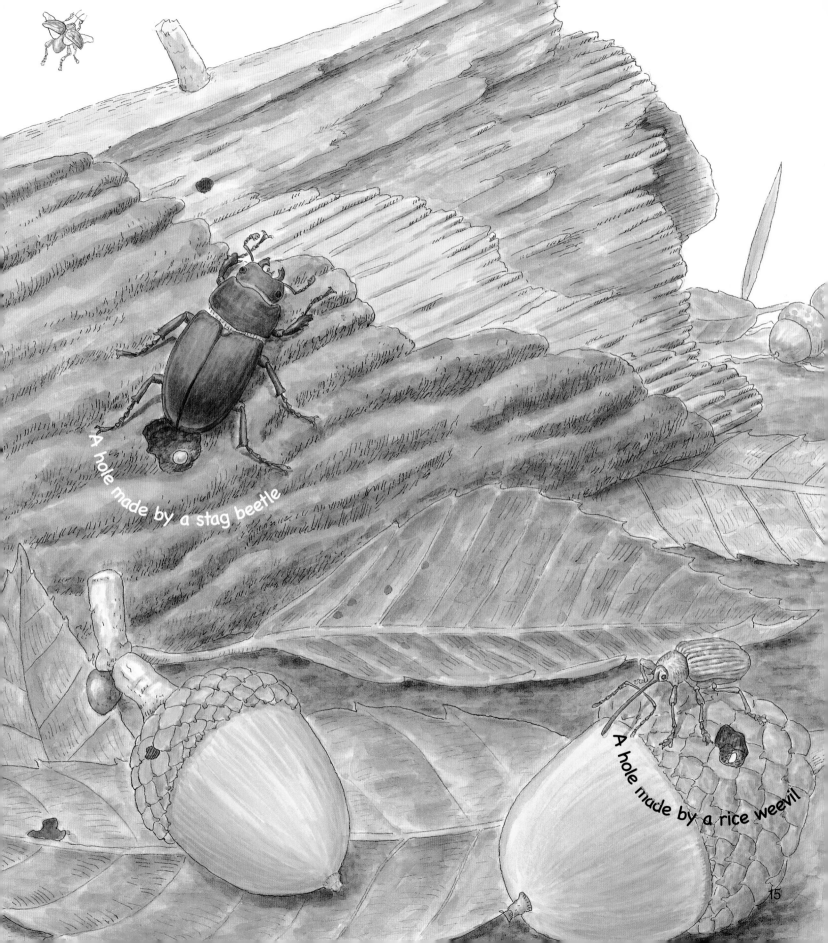

A hole made by a stag beetle

A hole made by a rice weevil

15

Holes are in the soft mud.
What made these holes?

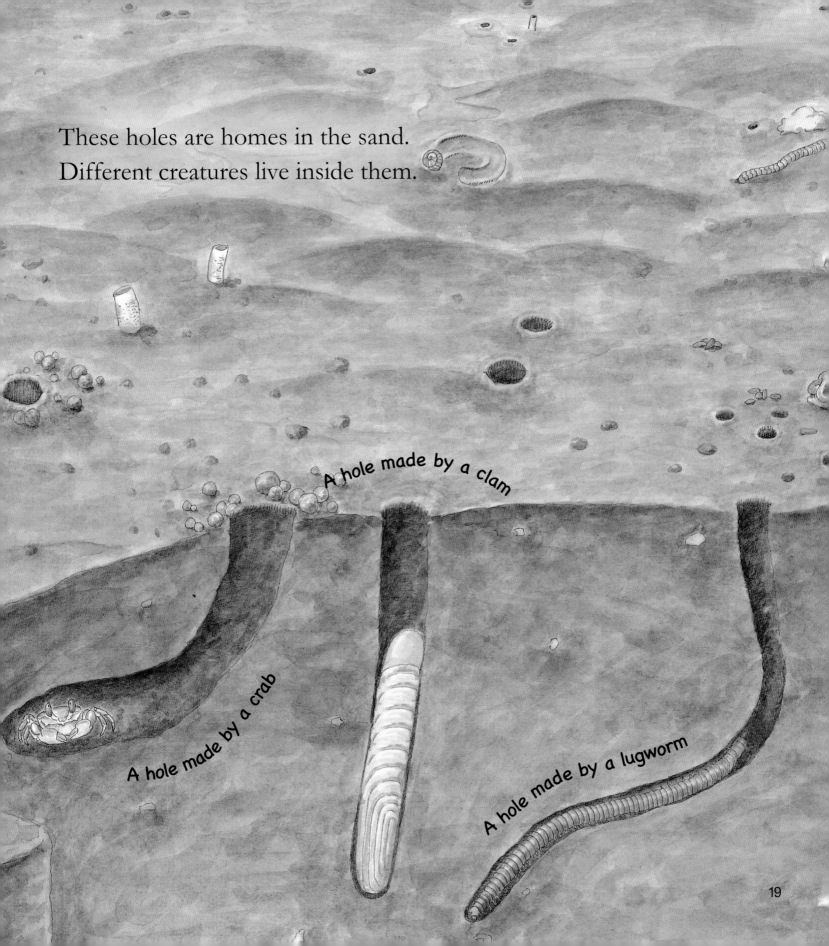

These holes are homes in the sand.
Different creatures live inside them.

A hole made by a clam

A hole made by a crab

A hole made by a lugworm

19

This hole, that hole!
What are these holes for?

In these cosy holes, creatures sleep through the winter.

A hole found by a bear

A hole dug by a frog

Here is a hole in a door.
What made it?

A mouse made that hole.
It can go in and out
through the hole.
It can hide from the cat.

A hole made by a mouse

So many holes!
What are they for?

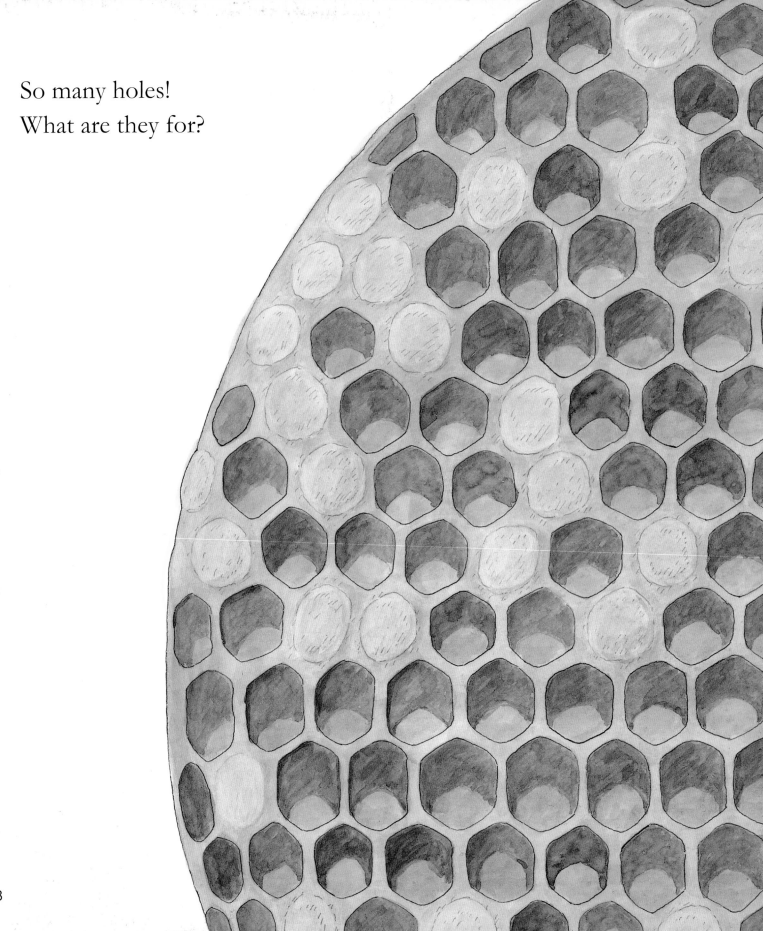

29

These holes are made by honeybees. The queen bee lays eggs in the holes. The eggs hatch and new larvae grow. They change into honeybees with wings. Then they can fly out into the air.

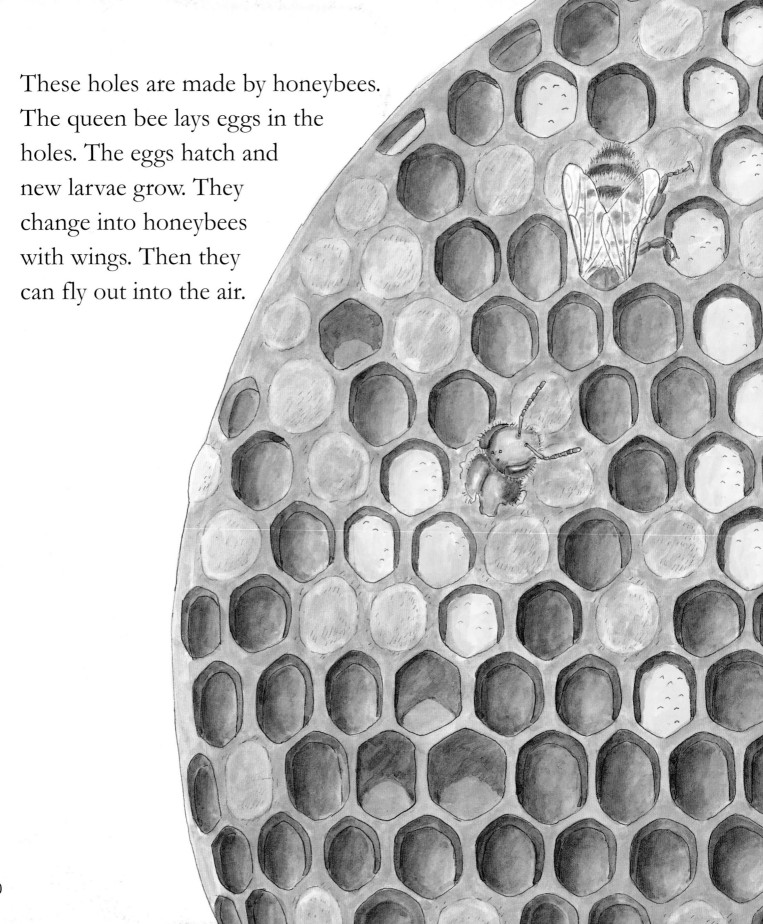

Holes filled with pollen

Holes with larvae

Hole with eggs

Holes filled with honey

This Hole, That Hole

There are many different types of holes in nature. Some animals make holes to find food. Other animals lay eggs in holes. And some animals live in holes. Let's find out what animals made these holes.

Let's think!

Why does a woodpecker make holes in trees?

How does a sow bug make a hole?

Why does a bear use a hole?

What do honeybees do with the holes they make?

Let's do!

Make some animal holes pictures! Use cutout pictures from magazines, construction paper, glue, scissors, and markers. Pick an animal from this book and make pictures of the animal and its hole. Label the pictures and write a fact about the animal too.